Starting Points

for

New Writers!

Jeri Darby

Jeri Darby

ISBN: 978-1-958811-11-5
Printed in the United States of America

Ararity Press
jeri@iamawriternow.com
989 402-4721

Facebook: Jeri Darby (Personal)
Facebook: I AM a Writer NOW! (Author)

Table of Contents

Dedication

This book is dedicated to each Writer
Who found the courage
To commit their wisdom and stories to
Printed pages.

"My tongue is the pen of a ready writer!"

Trust the Holy Spirit to get your story from
your tongue into your book!

I AM a Writer NOW!
Writing Declarations!

➢ The Spirit of the Lord is upon me, and He has anointed me to write.

➢ The Holy Spirit leads, guides, and instructs me on what I should write.

➢ I hear the voice of wisdom, I speak the voice of wisdom, I write the voice of wisdom.

➢ God shoots my books like arrows that hit His target audience with the words that He is releasing through me.

➢ I dismiss the lies of satan and BOLDLY proclaim that I AM a WRITER NOW!

➢ My readers report, "I couldn't put it down!" when reading my books.

➢ Whenever I put myself into a book, it destroys the works of the devil.

➢ God has people waiting for the release of my book(s).

➢ God sends my books to the four corners of the world to be a blessing to the families of the earth.

Introduction

"Where do I st----arrrrrrt!" I sense the agony released with this plea. This question emerges from every aspiring author that I have ever spoken with. Some bury their frustrations and never begin or lay aside the book they started for years. Others began their quest alone and get discouraged along the way because of insufficient or inaccurate information. It is common for writers to wrestle with starting, completing, and releasing their first book. Once done, the process becomes smoother for future adventures in writing.

Many woke up one day and sensed that a writer was trapped inside them and demanding to be released. This is not coincidental, but a divine act of God. If you are reading this book, you are well on the path to solving the *"where do I start"* riddle. Use this book as a tool and guide. It offers strategies that will facilitate your quest to become a published author. It is a stepping stone to jumpstart your writing process.

Recognizing effective starting points will make your transition from writer to author smoother. Utilize the approaches offered on these pages when beginning or continuing to write your book.

I am a Christian Author and Writing Coach. God has equipped me to activate, inspire and release the writer within others. There is an urgent demand for Christian Writers to come forth-*NOW!* God is covering the earth with His glory, and yours and the books of others is one of many ways that He's achieving His goal. Once I told people that "Writing was one of the most important assignments in the world." Then God corrected me saying, "Writing is *THE* most important assignment in the world!"

And yes, He entrusted you with this talent and is depending on you to complete His writing mission. This assignment was planted inside you before you were conceived in the womb. satan will attempt to detour you from every angle. Fight the good fight to focus, persevere and finish your writing course!

Resist the urge to compress your entire life into a single book. If writing a fictional story and it goes on and on and on… consider a series. Nothing says that you can only author one book. Once you commit to the writing process, other stories that are desperate to be written will attempt to hitch a ride in your book. Don't allow this to happen! It can take your book completely off course.

Keep a list of thoughts and titles for other books that present themselves and make a commitment to write them at a future date. Then, write them when the time is more suitable in a book that can better serve their purpose. You don't have to be a one-book wonder. Stretch your mind beyond writing a book—to writing books. This will decrease the temptation to squeeze in issues that do not fit into your current story.

Why?

Approaching the writing process with clarity is empowering. Use this space to clarify your *WHY?* Why do you feel called to write a book? Clarity is a weapon!

_____

_____

_____

_____

_____

_____

_____

_____

_____

_____

_____

_____

_____

_____

_____

_____

_____

_____

_____

_____

_____

_____

_____

_____

_____

_____

_____

_____

_____

_____

_____

_____

_____

_____

_____

_____

_____

_____

_____

_____

_____

_____

_____

_____

_____

_____

_____

Use the next pages to explore the direction you want to take your book. Write the vision, make it plain…

Targeting

Who? Audience:

Who are you writing for? Be specific. Identify one person in your target audience and write to that person. This could be a current or younger version of yourself… (age, struggles, gender, culture, race, education, student, financial, political, career, a person in the marketplace or church, entrepreneur, confidence issues, poor self-esteem, suicidal, married, addictions, chronic illness, divorced, widow, grieving, depressed, successful, history of failures) and so on…. Be clear to whom you are writing.

_____

_____

_____

_____

_____

_____

_____

What? Message:

Identify the message you want to impart to others through your book. Are you teaching a new skill? Are you imparting life principles or self-help? Weave your message into each chapter of your book.

_____

_____

_____

_____

When? Completion:

Writing a book takes commitment. It's one thing to start a book, and another to complete it. Set a realistic deadline and work towards it. Will you write in the mornings? Evenings? It would be nice to identify times and places to complete your writing commitment. You may not find large blocks of time to write or have a special place. Begin with just 15 minutes a day. Explore writing in different environments. You will be surprised at what can be accomplished with 15 minutes of daily focused writing. Engage in regular writing routines to ensure your success.

_____

_____

_____

_____

How?

Will you write with pen and paper? Will you type on a device? Either is fine. Discover what works best for you. If you choose to handwrite your story. Plan to have it typed before hiring an editor. It is a challenge to find an editor that will accept handwritten books. Some services will transcribe it for a fee if needed.

_____

_____

_____

_____

Genre:

Fiction, nonfiction, romance, drama, spiritual, or business, there are many ways to present your story. I write primarily non-fiction, but I venture into other forms of writing. You will never know how far-reaching your writing gift is—until you stretch. Your story can be created in different forms. Such as a book, play, movie script, or TV Series. Dare to explore ways to expand your talent. Don't compare or compete with others. Pray and ask God for specific directions and embrace your uniqueness.

_____

_____

_____

_____

_____

Invest time to consider each of the previous sections to gain greater clarity of the book you are about to write. Avoid stagnation. Keep moving forward!

_____

_____

_____

_____

Life Experiences/Stories

List the various roles you have experienced during your life's journey, daughter, sister, brother, husband, and wife. Include education, training, skills, depression, abuses, divorce, achievements, disappointments, traumas, and physical conditions. You may or may not include these things in your book—prayerfully consider what to integrate. This exercise can also help you to further identify and target your audiences. Don't be surprised if you find things surfacing that you have long forgotten. List cues for personal stories you may want to include in your book.

_____   _____
_____   _____
_____   _____
_____   _____
_____   _____
_____   _____
_____   _____
_____   _____
_____   _____
_____   _____
_____   _____
_____   _____
_____   _____
_____   _____
_____   _____
_____   _____
_____   _____
_____   _____
_____   _____
_____   _____

Chapters, Titles, and Subtitles

It will be easier to write your book once you envision chapters. I have received numerous manuscripts Needing organization and chapter division, it is quite challenging. I recommend that you think in terms of chapters to help organize your book. If trying to conceive chapters gets you stuck. Just write! You can create chapters later. Do at some point identify, separate and give your chapters a title. Use the Mind Mapping tools to help you visualize different aspects of your book.

Mind Mapping

Chapter Development

This is another way to organize your thoughts before writing. There are several ways that this method can be utilized. Use extra paper or the space on the right side of the page to draw more circles if needed.

1-Use the middle square to place the topic of your book. Use ovals to place chapter topics.

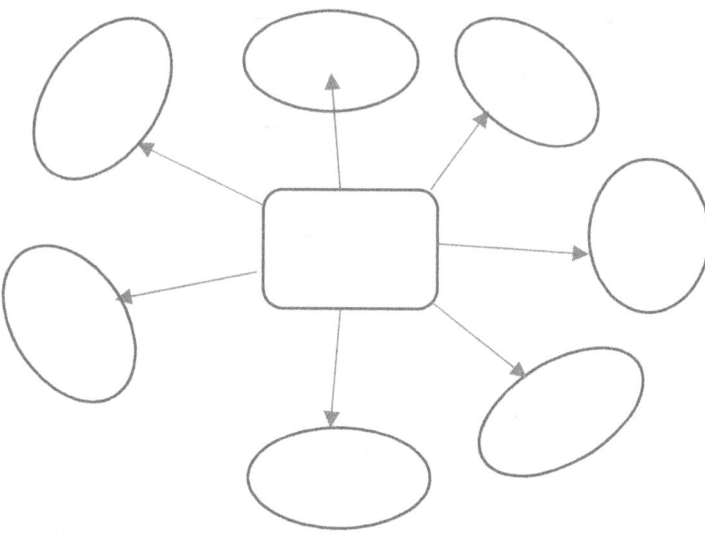

Paragraph Construction

2-Use the middle square to place the topic of one of your book chapters. Use ovals to place issues you want to address in each paragraph.

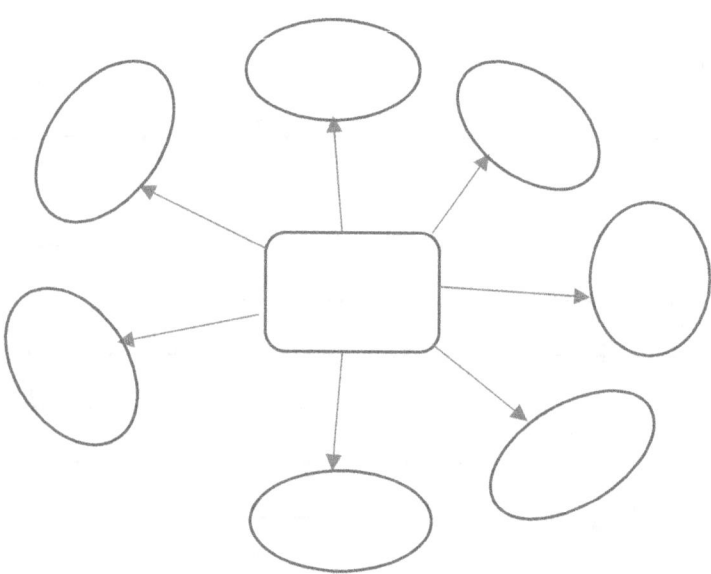

Mind Mapping

Chapter Development

This is another way to organize your thoughts before writing. There are several ways that this method can be utilized. Use extra paper or the space on the right side of the page to draw more circles if needed.

   1-Use the middle square to place the topic of your book. Use ovals to place chapter topics.

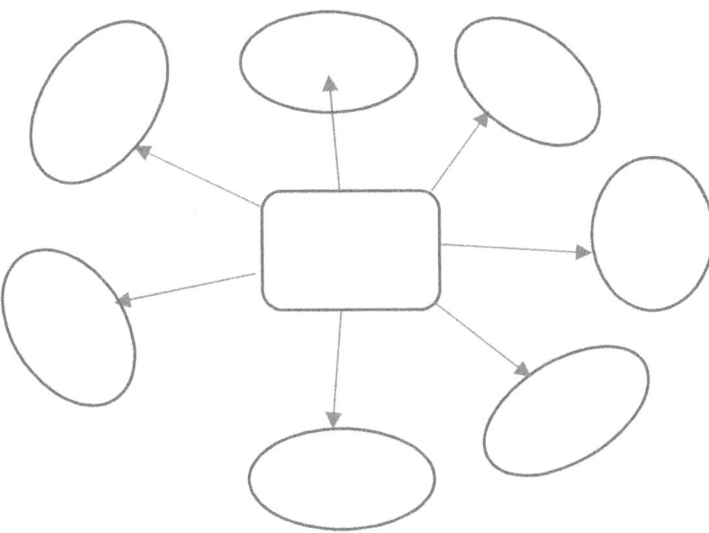

Paragraph Construction

2-Use the middle square to place the topic of one of your book chapters. Use ovals to place issues you want to address in each paragraph.

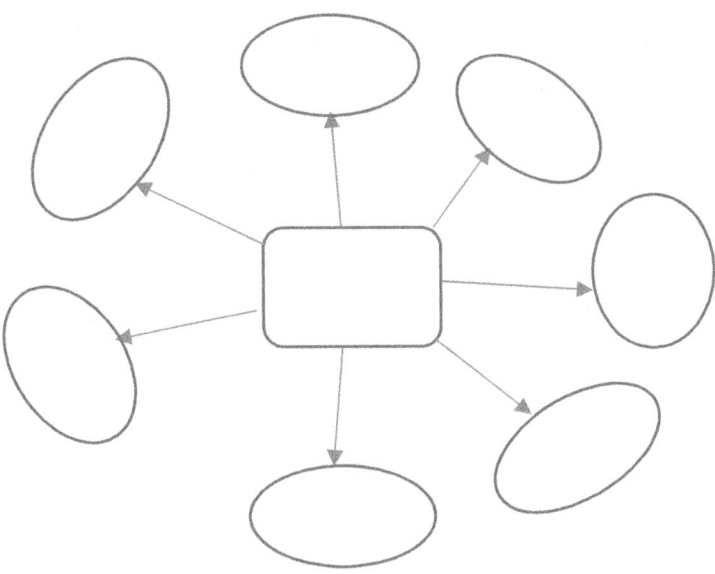

Topic Development

3-Use the middle square to place the topic of one of your book chapters. Use ovals to place issues you want to address in each paragraph.

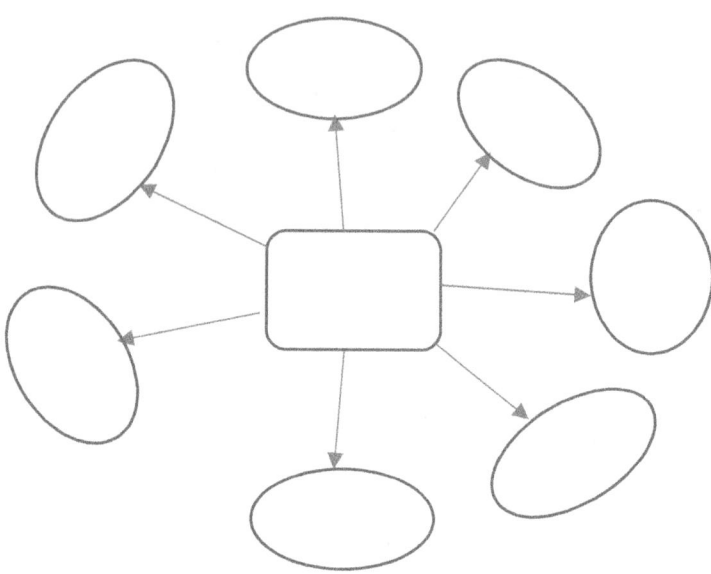

Title Considerations

4-Use the middle square to place the topic of one of your books. Use ovals to brainstorm tentative titles.

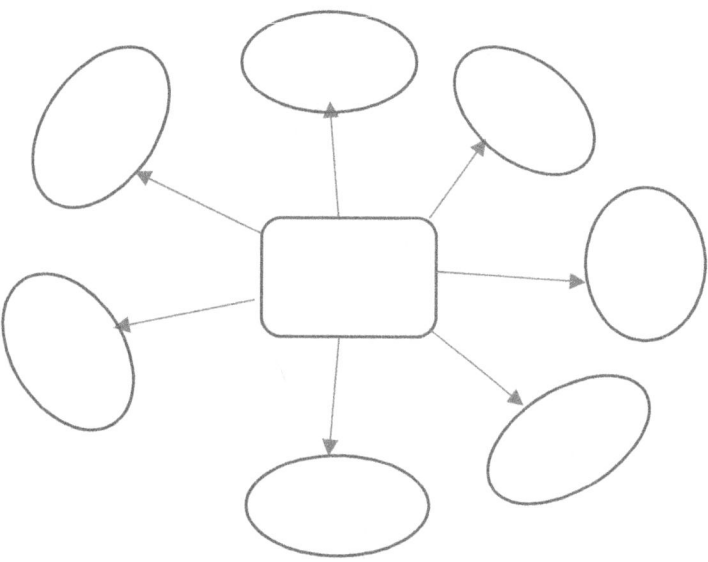

Topic Development

3-Use the middle square to place the topic of one of your book chapters. Use ovals to place issues you want to address in each paragraph.

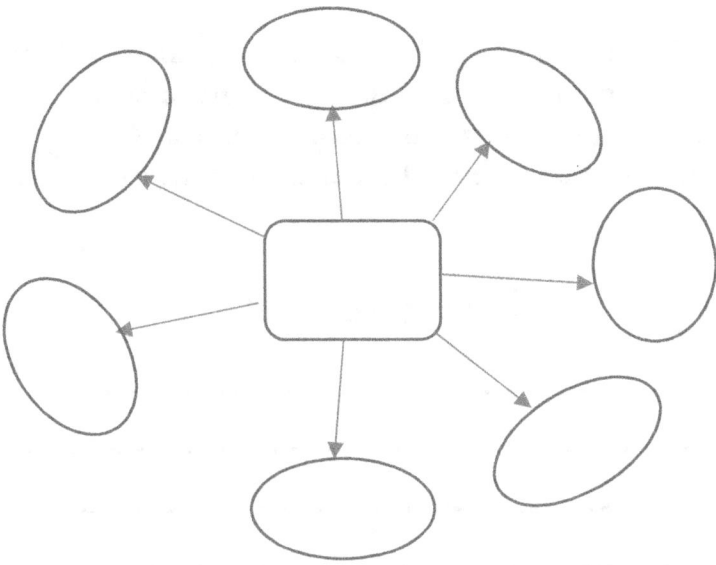

Title Considerations

4-Use the middle square to place the topic of one of your books. Use ovals to brainstorm tentative titles.

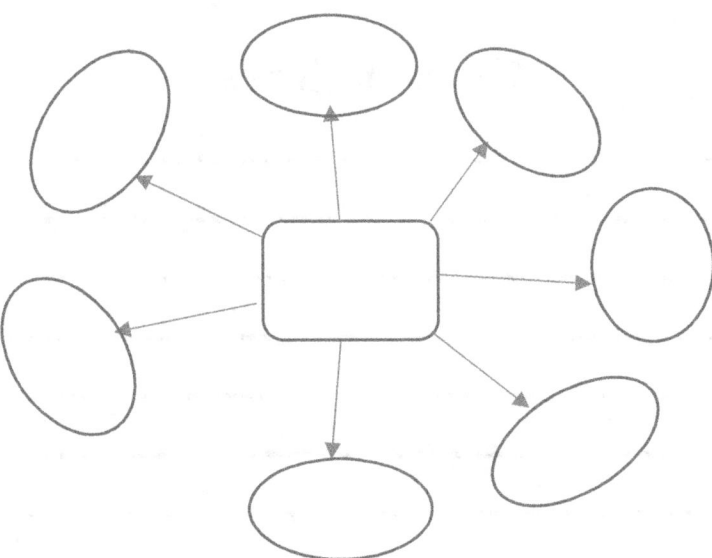

Character Development

Use this section to explore names for your characters. List tentative names on the left and add more details on the left. Example male/female, age, roles (son, daughter, student, married, divorced, widowed, income range etc...)

Include unique traits or physical, emotional, or other challenges that your character may be facing.

If writing a nonfiction book, you can use this section to help clarify what you wish to include in your story about each person you are writing about. Actual names can be fictionalized when you wish to protect to privacy of the person you are writing about. This can also be done when writing about yourself. You can share your personal experience under a fictional name.

Name   Characteristics

_____   _____
                                 _____
                                 _____
                                 _____
                                 _____
                                 _____
                                 _____

Name   Characteristics

_____   _____
                                 _____
                                 _____
                                 _____
                                 _____
                                 _____

Name

Characteristics

_____

_____

_____

_____

_____

_____

_____

Name

Characteristics

_____

_____

_____

_____

_____

_____

_____

Name

Characteristics

_____

_____

_____

_____

_____

_____

_____

Name   **Characteristics**

_____

_____

_____

_____

_____

_____

_____

Name   **Characteristics**

_____

_____

_____

_____

_____

_____

_____

Name   **Characteristics**

_____

_____

_____

_____

_____

_____

_____

Name   **Characteristics**

_____   _____

                                   _____

                                   _____

                                   _____

                                   _____

                                   _____

                                   _____

Name   **Characteristics**

_____   _____

                                   _____

                                   _____

                                   _____

                                   _____

                                   _____

                                   _____

Name   **Characteristics**

_____   _____

                                   _____

                                   _____

                                   _____

                                   _____

                                   _____

                                   _____

How to Use Chapter Pages

Use the following pages to make a brief draft of what you desire to include in your chapters.

Use the information that you placed in the mind mapping section.

These pages can be used to take notes as more ideas come about developing each chapter.

It's important to empty your mind of the current ideas that you have in mind.

If you don't you risk the same thoughts circling in your head. Release them, so new ones can emerge.

So, if your downloads come here a little and there a little, jot them down in the appropriate chapter.

Dedication/Quote/Scripture etc.

Acknowledgment
(Write about those you want to acknowledge here.)

_____

_____

_____

_____

_____

_____

_____

_____

_____

_____

_____

_____

_____

_____

_____

_____

_____

_____

_____

_____

_____

Chapter _____

_____

_____

_____

_____

_____

_____

_____

_____

_____

_____

_____

_____

_____

_____

_____

_____

_____

_____

_____

_____

_____

_____

_____

_____

_____

_____

_____

_____

Chapter _____

_____

_____

_____

_____

_____

_____

_____

_____

_____

_____

_____

_____

_____

_____

_____

_____

_____

_____

_____

_____

_____

_____

_____

_____

_____

_____

Chapter _____

_____
_____
_____
_____
_____
_____
_____
_____
_____
_____
_____
_____
_____
_____
_____
_____
_____
_____
_____
_____
_____
_____
_____
_____
_____
_____
_____
_____

Chapter _____

Chapter _____

_____

_____

_____

_____

_____

_____

_____

_____

_____

_____

_____

_____

_____

_____

_____

_____

_____

_____

_____

_____

_____

_____

_____

_____

_____

_____

_____

_____

_____

Chapter _____

_____

_____

_____

_____

_____

_____

_____

_____

_____

_____

_____

_____

_____

_____

_____

_____

_____

_____

_____

_____

_____

_____

_____

_____

_____

_____

_____

Chapter _____

_____
_____
_____
_____
_____
_____
_____
_____
_____
_____
_____
_____
_____
_____
_____
_____
_____
_____
_____
_____
_____
_____
_____
_____
_____
_____
_____
_____

Chapter _____

_____

_____

_____

_____

_____

_____

_____

_____

_____

_____

_____

_____

_____

_____

_____

_____

_____

_____

_____

_____

_____

_____

_____

_____

_____

Chapter _____

Chapter _____

Chapter _____

Chapter _____

Chapter _____

Chapter _____

Chapter _____

_____
_____
_____
_____
_____
_____
_____
_____
_____
_____
_____
_____
_____
_____
_____
_____
_____
_____
_____
_____
_____
_____
_____
_____
_____
_____
_____
_____
_____
_____

Chapter _____

Chapter _____

_____

_____

_____

_____

Chapter _____

About the Author
(Tell your readers about yourself.)

_____

_____

_____

_____

_____

_____

_____

_____

_____

_____

_____

_____

_____

_____

_____

_____

_____

_____

_____

_____

_____

_____

_____

_____

_____

Back of Book

Write a blurb on the back of your book needs to snag enough of the reader's curiosity so they will open and explore it further and decide to purchase. Make it exciting & engaging!

_____

_____

_____

_____

_____

_____

_____

_____

_____

_____

_____

_____

_____

_____

_____

_____

_____

_____

_____

_____

_____

_____

_____

Your Writing Process

Do you write in the mornings at 5 am? Do you write one thousand words each day? Do you write at the same time and in the same place? There are many books written offering strategies of when, where, how, and how long you should write to experience success. I have struggled and failed miserably while attempting to attain some of these lofty goals.

I master a set of instructions for a *brief* season. Then I start feeling like a fish trying to fly. Attempting to master a skill that's beyond my capability. There were times when life thrust me into seasons of difficulties. There were times when I was distracted and did not write for years. Non-writing is agonizing for a true writer!

Like me, perhaps your writing practices may never achieve the level of discipline recommended by many successful authors. This does not mean that you cannot be a success. Life has trained me to write *whenever, wherever* and *however* I can. I suggest you do the same. If your writing schedule happens to fall into neatly organized slots, spaces, and places—great! If not—these are not valid reasons not to write.

Reading and writing are my first loves. The demands of life routinely crowd them out. Everyone seems to be in a hurry, racing through life, rushing to get from here to there—including me. Sometimes I purposely slow down and take ten. While sitting in the car, I read or write ten minutes before completing my shopping or other errands. You will be amazed at how this minimal level of commitment can help you complete your book.

Too often, we opt out of starting our book because we cannot carve out a large chunk of uninterrupted writing time. Here a little, there a little. With determination and consistency, you can complete your book! The important thing is to maintain an intimate connection with writing and to keep moving forward.

Distractions will surely come; write through them! Commitment to small segments of time regularly accomplishes much—it will astonish you! Dismiss lying voices today challenging your worthiness to be a writer by declaring into the atmosphere I AM a WRITER NOW!"

Writing Tips

1. The rules have changed! Just one space after a $(.)$

2. Avoid redundancy, eg, stand-up, sit-down, bald-headed. The only way you can stand is up, or sit is down, and bald generally refers to the head.

3. Avoid extremely long sentences. Google "empty words" to obtain a list of words and phrases to avoid. Wordiness slows the pace of your writing, e.g., "It's important, in order to, as a matter of fact, you must... to tell the truth, In my opinion," etc.... This weakens your writing. Also, avoid words like very, really, actually...

4. Complete your book before attempting to edit. One side of your brain creates while the other wants to fix constantly. Attempting to fix it before it is done will only get you stuck.

5. Don't marry your draft. The first writing is *never* ready to be published! Self-edit. Rewrite to the best of your ability *before* getting it to an editor.

6. When hiring an editor, ask what type of editing they will perform. Spelling and punctuation alone will not elevate your book to a publishable level. There are more than 15 types of editing processes.

7. Check reviews for coaches, editors, publishers, etc. Many writers are discouraged because of negative experiences with providers of writing services.

8. Write through distractions…they may be something to include in your book. To a writer…EVERYTHING…is potential writing material.

9. Writing Prompts-Google and use writing prompts to stretch your writing mind or get through dry spells. You will be amazed at what erupts!

10. Write like you talk. Avoid overusing big words. Research shows that many adults read on a 7th or 8th-grade level.

11. Identify an accountability partner to share your progress, and voice your frustrations. Offer mutual support and prayer.

12. Just write! Don't worry about making corrections—fix it later.

13. Write past the negative voices. Satan will do everything within his power to convince you that your story is trash—Remember—**SATAN IS A LIAR!**

14. Boldly proclaim to others EVERY DAY! "I AM a Writer NOW!

15. Jesus is the Author and Finisher of your faith. The Holy Spirit is your Personal Assistant and an Amazing Writer! Pray, Listen, and Trust His direction.

Write Your Introduction

Writing your introduction can navigate you through the starting gate. It may give you the momentum you need to dive into your story. Sometimes, introductions are written after the completion of your book. This is one method to consider. There are various ways to write a great introduction.

1. Begin with the *problem* your book will address.

2. *Share what makes you credible.* What qualifies you to write this book? Not based on your education or the initials behind your name. What life experiences qualify you?

3. Tell *how* your book is going to address the problem.

4. Make the reader feel like they are missing out on vital information if they choose to bypass your book!

_____

_____

_____

_____

_____

_____

_____

_____

_____

_____

_____

_____

_____

_____

_____

_____

_____

_____

But I Don't Feel Like Writing!

"I have to write; this is how I make my living." I have heard this spoken more than once by seasoned writers who spoke at conferences. Nothing invigorates a writer like a good writing conference! It's like jumpstarting a car with a dead battery. No, you will not always feel like writing. Words will not always readily flow. Many succumb to discouragement during writing droughts and give up, "I have writer's block," is how this dry season is explained.

You can place a demand on your words to flow. Just like we walk by faith, and not by sight, the same goes with writing. We write by faith and not by feelings. I don't think that writing can be blocked, though sometimes you may have to give your words time to warm up when you first sit to write.

Imagine walking into the bathroom and getting ready to take a bath or shower. You turn on the faucet, but nothing runs out but cold water! You don't panic and forfeit your bath. Experience has taught you that if you let it run long enough—it will get hot. Depending on the effectiveness of its heating source, the water could quickly become scalding!

The same thing happens when writing. I have begun writing ventures with words like, "I don't know what to write about today, or I don't feel like writing today..." I keep letting the cold words run. Before I know it I write something that sounds profound! To me, anyway. 😊 I read it again while wondering where did that come from? The temperature changes, and the flow of my words has gone from cold to sizzling!

Even if your words don't reach a scorching point that day—continue to write—they will! Remember, your first copy is just a draft; it does not need to be perfect. When you read through it a second time, you will have greater clarity on anything you need to add or change to improve. The important thing is to get your book done!

The next section will include space for you to engage in writing prompts. Engage in practices that allow you opportunities to stretch your writing gift beyond your comfort zone. Devout 10-15 minutes to these endeavors.

Do it with another person or in a group. Then, read your results aloud to each other. It's fun! Like me, you may be surprised to discover that your writing talent surpasses anything you ever thought or imagined! Write when you feel like it, write when you don't. Place a demand on your words to flow! This is what real writers do!

Don't Marry Your Draft

The Power of the Re-write!

Too often authors type that final period on their manuscript and rush it off to an editor. Healthy books are seldom produced this way. The first level of editing needs to be done by you—the writer. We often hear a book referred to as a birthing process. I receive some books demanding intense editing to be viable. I feel like a surrogate with books implanted inside my writing womb.

It takes labor amongst the writer, editor, and publisher to release a healthy book. Many writers when done rush their book to an editor, without a second glance. "It is finished!" they announce, overwhelmed with excitement. Some of these manuscripts have been shelved for years. "Can this be published next month?"

The book has suddenly achieved 911 status! I no longer accept manuscripts with urgent completion deadlines. Editing, formatting, and publishing are detailed processes. Unforeseen glitches and delays occur. Some are unavoidable, others are aimed at improving the quality of your end product.

Don't trust that another person is going to perceive your book with the same love and passion as you. If you feel that you are incapable of doing an adequate job of self-editing, ask a qualified family or friend. Offer compensation if need be. There are self-editing approaches that can be valuable.

This has been the single most helpful technique for me when it comes to self-editing. Reading along while listening to my story captures not only errors but helps with identifying needed changes in the organization and flow of a manuscript. I accidentally discovered that my computer would read aloud to me! Oh, happy day! This has revolutionized my editing approach for myself and my clients. I am listening, editing, and re-writing this session in preparation for uploading today. While listening you can hear the pace, rhythm, and inflections clearer than by reading alone; as well as picking up things that are missed when just reading.

If "read aloud," is not included in the Word program on your device, this feature is offered on Google Drive. YouTube instructions for use on your phone or other devices. Listening to your writing offers insights into beneficial changes. I know, it sounds like more work. It is—but so—ooo worth it!

Each writer must determine the amount of time and effort they are willing to invest to elevate their book to its highest potential. Your book has the possibility to be read, quoted, and impact the lives of others for ongoing generations! Within the scope of your abilities make it the best that it can be, before passing it on to an editor!

I am not talking about a never-ending editing process to produce the *perfect* book. There are no perfect books! My coach says, "done is better than perfect." I agree. Each book I've written or produced for others has been a learning process and a stepping stone toward improving my coaching and publishing strategies. If you plan to embrace the writing mantle long-term, continue to learn and grow in the art of writing and self-editing. I have never written anything that didn't shine brighter after rewriting.

Writing was the easy part. Re-writing is the place where great books are born! In this place, you will recognize strategies and new thoughts that will elevate your book. Guess what? I am re-writing this session right now, and I am going to self-edit once more. ☺ I want you to hear what I am saying with your writer's heart! Otherwise, your emotions will kick in with something like, "Are you kidding me? I am *not* doing all that extra work! That's what editors are for!" I've been there!

If that's what you are hearing, shut it down! Look for ways to make your story more engaging. Consider whether portions need to be added—or excluded. Your editor may capture some of the blind spots—they may not. Polish your book to the best of your ability is all I'm saying. At least commit to these basic principles:

1. If it is the end of a sentence, use a period, question mark, or whatever is appropriate.

2. Break your writing into paragraphs. Don't go page after page without a break. A good editor will adjust paragraphing as needed.

3. If it is supposed to be capital—do it!

Such simple omissions can require an editor to be alert for over a thousand changes—depending on the length of your book. This is no exaggeration, been there—done that! This is time-consuming and could prove costly. It also distracts from other forms of editing that would add the greatest value to your book.

Your book is your baby, and it needs to be dressed with the best presentation that you can offer before passing it on. I understand, I get books that after the writer has done their best—it is not publishable when presented to me. I am gifted at fixing this—as I am sure others are also, but this does increase editing costs. I will no longer quote an editing fee for a client without reviewing a minimum of one chapter of their book.

There are many approaches to the editing process. Some editors provide basic services, which include spelling, punctuation, and grammar. Most books require an editing approach beyond this level to be publishable. By "publishable," I mean a book that someone will actually read following publication. Book sales are important, but having someone tell you, "That I could not put it down," when referring to *your* book—is priceless. Explore what it will take for you to produce a healthy book. Pray for God's direction and trust the process he lays out for you. It may not look like everyone else's—it's okay. I don't compare my coaching approach with that of others—it works for me.

I am a Production Editor. This type of editing involves evaluating a manuscript's targeting, engagement, flow, organization, and more. I receive manuscripts that sometimes require over a thousand editing corrections for basic issues. Writers seldom appreciate the in-depth commitment involved with editing. I interview writers when needed to fill holes in their stories that may leave readers cliff-hanging in confusion.

When that first draft is completed, the excitement is contagious! The last thing you want to hear is, "Write it over!" But this is the only way you will discover the true depth of your writing talent. Some books require editing surgery to cut away tumors—an overgrowth of words that do not belong in that book. Others need liposuction to remove the excess fat, weighing down the impact of their message.

During one writing conference, an editor shared that he received a handwritten book submission. The writer included a letter saying, "I have written this book exactly as God gave it to me; please do not change anything." He went on to describe all the basic mistakes made throughout. Mistakes are common for new writers because we don't know what we don't know. If you set out to be a piano player, you would not just start playing and expect to excel without further training. So, it is with writing.

Investing time in self-editing demonstrates to yourself and your book that this project is important. Once you align yourself with God's purpose, He continually transforms your life from glory to glory. You can do the same with your book. Partner with Holy Spirit while creating your book. When you are done, put it aside for a while, and when you resume, examine areas that would benefit from a re-write.

Return with fresh eyes and you will see things that were not apparent before. Search for changes that will elevate your story. I was recently reading my first book, "Stepping Stones, Reflections for Singles."

"Wow! This is good writing!" I recall thinking this. Though I laid this book aside for twenty years before publishing, I self-edited, polished, and scrubbed it many times before it was ever released. No, re-writing need not take years. It is a worthy venture.

Creation is a powerful process. Trust it. Use capitals, periods, and paragraphs when indicated if you have such skills. If not ask someone to do general proofreading. An editor can and does address these issues. Yet the less time an editor spends on making basic changes, the more time can be devoted to other details such as the flow, organization, and chapter development. Attention to these areas will take your book to new levels and increase the reader's engagement. You can purchase my video series to help with your self-editing process titled, "Starting Points for New Writers!" Email me at jeri@iamawriternow.com for details.

No Hitchhiking Allowed!

Okay! You are finally writing! Excited? Guess who else is excited? The author that has awakened inside you. Now that your creativity has been jolted, it may feel like you are exploding with writing ideas. These concepts may try to hitch a ride in a book that you are working on, even if you are not headed in its direction.

This doesn't mean that they lack the promising potential to be something profound. But it will only ambush the story and detour your original goal. Don't leave the hitchhikers stranded. This section provides a safe space for new book titles, stories, movies, plays, etc. to rest until your mind is free to give them the attention they deserve.

Drop them off here and promise to come back to get them when your creativity is traveling in their direction. Now that the author in you has been unleashed permit yourself to own your identity as a WRITER! As AUTHOR! Writers, WRITE! Not just a single book, but ALL the books crying out to be released through them.

Record Your New Writing Ideas

_____

_____

_____

_____

_____

_____

_____

_____

_____

_____

_____

_____

Writing Prompt Exercise

Google "Writing Prompts." Use these blank lines for writing exercises. Writing prompts can trigger new thoughts, and new materials and take your writing journey in new directions, and so on. They are great practice to increase your skills!

_____
_____
_____
_____
_____
_____
_____
_____
_____
_____
_____
_____
_____
_____
_____
_____
_____
_____
_____
_____
_____
_____
_____
_____
_____
_____
_____

More Writing Prompt Exercise

Google "Writing Prompts." Use these blank lines for writing exercises. Writing prompts can trigger new thoughts, and new materials that take your writing journey in new directions, and so on. They are great practice to increase your skills!

_____
_____
_____
_____
_____
_____
_____
_____
_____
_____
_____
_____
_____
_____
_____
_____
_____
_____
_____
_____
_____
_____
_____
_____
_____
_____
_____
_____

More Writing Prompt Exercise

Google "Writing Prompts." Use these blank lines for writing exercises. Writing prompts can trigger new thoughts, new materials and take your writing journey in new directions, and so on. They are great practice to increase your skills!

_____

_____

_____

_____

_____

_____

_____

_____

_____

_____

_____

_____

_____

_____

_____

_____

_____

_____

_____

_____

_____

_____

_____

_____

_____

_____

Author's Note

I purposely excluded information about the publishing process because I want you to focus on writing your book. When God first spoke to me about writing a book, just like you, I did not know where to start. "I will have someone to help you get to the next place whenever you are ready." This is how God responded to my despondency. He kept His word. Whenever I am ready to move to a new level, God always sends someone to help with my advancement.

He will be there for you also.

There is enormous competition among writing coaches and publishers for the financial investment of those desiring to become authors. Some services are costly and deliver little, others are less expensive and deliver much, and there's everything in between. Let God, not the cost, make your final decision. A woman connected with me when she was ready to publish her book. "Do you charge?" She asked. When I confirmed that I did, she decided to go with someone who would train her to publish her own book.

My heart grieved when I saw the finished product. It did not do justice to her powerful story! Again, be prayerful and not led by emotions or finances. Many writers have become discouraged and abandoned their writing pursuits because of disappointing services from coaches and/or publishers. They trusted those who failed to deliver the desired outcome. I have worked with clients who paid other coaches, other editors, and other publishers and were displeased with the end product and were willing to pay to go through the process again with me.

Once the decision is made to complete your book, guard against impulsivity and jumping at glamorous ads offering publishing services. Many coaches and publishers are doing an outstanding job. Beware of those who have published one book and soon afterward offer to edit or publish your book. They may be fabulous! We all start somewhere but seek God for direction.

I don't chase after clients. I realize that I am not for everyone. It is important to work with someone that's a "good fit" for my style of coaching. I pray and ask God to send writers to me that He has designated for me to assist with their publishing journey. I am unapologetically a Christian Writing Coach; I never want to be responsible for helping to publish something that will deter someone from God's path. I have declined to work with some for this reason. Satan has perverted the writing gifts of many, and he has ample books, movies, etc., etc. penetrating the media.

It is time for God's army of writers to arise and even the warzone! Meanwhile, don't isolate yourself during this journey. Writers are guilty of this. Use this next section to collect information on contacts. Don't you hate scrambling through notebooks, scraps of paper, and napkins trying to retrieve information for someone you want to connect with? Use this space to capture people, websites, FB writing groups, coaches, publishers, etc., that you would like to learn more about. There is much to learn about the journey of becoming an author. Don't try to assimilate it all at once.

Make your list as you write. God will lead you into the next phase, the next contact, the next strategy. He has not given you the unction to write a book, only to leave you clueless. Follow Him, and whatever He says, do it! I pray that this workbook has been a tool to get unstuck. God is trusting His writers to leave the messages that He has engraved upon our hearts upon the earth. Your God-ordained book will be a blessing to the children of men!

Notes

Use the following pages to record useful information for your ongoing
publishing process.

_____

_____

_____

_____

_____

_____

_____

_____

_____

_____

_____

_____

_____

_____

_____

_____

_____

_____

_____

_____

_____

_____

_____

_____

_____

NOTES

NOTES _____

NOTES _____

_____

_____

_____

_____

_____

_____

_____

_____

_____

_____

_____

_____

_____

_____

_____

_____

_____

_____

_____

_____

_____

_____

_____

_____

_____

_____

_____

_____

_____

_____

_____

A Writer's Prayer

Lord, I am Your scribe…
Let the Creativity of the
Holy Spirit flow…Unimpeded
Carrying the Power of Your
Light and Truth.
Be glorified & let those
Who read be elevated,
To a new place of
Faith, Hope & Love…

You ARE the Author
&
Finisher of my faith.
Today, I embrace my Author's identity,
I welcome divine writing assignments.
Before you planted me inside
My mother's womb,
I was called to write.
I trust you with all my heart.

Holy Spirit, empower me to release
A written word that will become,
Bread to the hungry,
Water to the thirsty,
Keys to those imprisoned.
I humble myself before your Mighty Hand
That You may exalt me in due season
To arise, Your anointed Scribe.
In Jesus's Name,

Amen

Certificate of Completion

Name:

_____

On this date: _____

I Boldly Proclaim:

I AM a Writer NOW!

About the Author

Jeri Darby is an Author Speaker and writing Coach. She has over thirty years of writing experiences with magazines and self-publishing. The "Where do I start question," is the most asked when speaking with beginning writers.

Like a midwife, Jeri has helped struggling writers to embrace their author's identity and birth their books. She utilizes a coaching approach that activates, inspire, and releases the author trapped within.

Jeri published her first book at age sixty-two and has plans to write one hundred. She loves to see the light shining on the face of a new author while embracing their book. Jeri had a dream that she died and went to heaven. She stood awaiting to hear the words, "well done!" Instead, God and the Angels looked perplexed.

A heavy silence filled the air, then God spoke. "What are you doing up here with all those books inside you? We do not need your books up here. You were supposed to leave those on the earth!" I awoke with a new urgency to release the numerous books waiting to be released from my creative womb.

Jeri has known many aspiring authors who die without releasing their books. She is thankful that God utilizes her years of writing knowledge to serve others. Jeri is a Production Editor. This type of editing goes beyond spelling and grammar.

Jeri's editing includes assessing the flow, organization, and tone of your book. She assesses for clarity and targeting. Jeri provides creative input that will cause your book to be more engaging making a greater impact on readers.

I AM a Writer NOW! Coaching Service imparts prayer, encouragement, and new knowledge to her clients to empower them to continue their journey of writing on a higher level.

Companion Book

I Am a Writer NOW!

30 Day Devotional
Motivation for Writers

Can serve as a companion book to Starting Points...
These 30 inspirational readings will fuel the writer in you while
completing your book!

New Release
In a Snap! 28 Inspirational Stories of Answered Prayer

Other Titles by Jeri Darby

Available on Amazon
or
Website: www.iamawriternow.com

Coming in Spanish
Soon!

Thank You for Reading

Starting Points for New Writers!
Watch for more new titles by Jeri Darby this year…

Your Amazon and/or Facebook Review
is appreciated!

The greatest way to support an Author
Is to complete a review and/or share your experience with
their book with others 😊

Blessings!

Need a Writing Coach?
Schedule your free consultation today!
Contact Information…989 402-4721

Jeri Darby
Visit My Online Bookstore at www.iamawriternow.com
jeri@iamawriternow.com
989 402-4721

www.ingramcontent.com/pod-product-compliance
Lightning Source LLC
Chambersburg PA
CBHW081008120626

46546CB00010B/3063